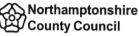
…es …lagee was born in Greenock, Scotland, and worked as a teacher and head teacher for many years before be……ing a full-time author in 1989. He writes his poe…s, plays, and stories in an old caravan at the bottom …… large (and wild) garden high up on the North York …s.

…indberg is an illustrator and writer. Her children's …… include *Robotina Finds Out* and *Creepy Kokey*. …s worked for the *Independent,* the *Guardian* and … 3C. She loves travelling and writing about it. Her …ave included sailing in a Tall Ships Race to Lisbon, …ing to Elf School in Iceland. She lives with robots …nd-up toys, and has a daughter called Emerald.

# THE VERY BEST OF...

# WES MAGEE

## A Book of Poems

Illustrated by Sally Kindberg

MACMILLAN CHILDREN'S BOOKS

*For all the Magees – past and present*

First published 2001
by Macmillan Children's Books

This edition produced 2002 for
The Book People Ltd, Hall Wood Avenue,
Haydock, St Helens WA11 9UL

ISBN 0 330 48192 4

3 5 7 9 8 6 4

A CIP catalogue record for this book is available from the British Library.

Printed by Mackays of Chatham plc, Chatham, Kent.

# Contents

# Introduction

In 1970, when I was a teacher, a boy in my class (Park North Junior School, Swindon) said, 'Mr Magee, I can't find any poems about dinosaurs.' When I searched through the school's poetry books I realized the boy was right: there were no such poems.

Although I'd never written for children I decided to try creating verse about such beasts as Diplodocus, Stegosaurus, and Dimetrodon. That weekend I completed seven poems, took them into school, and handed them to the pupils in my class. 'Hey, these poems are quite good!' a girl said. That was the start for me as a children's author.

Today, I look back on more than seventy publications for young readers – books of poems, plays, and stories. You'd think by now I'd find it easy to write a new book. Not a bit of it! It's always unnerving (scary, even) to stare at a blank page (or computer screen) wondering what to write. Somehow or other a new idea enters my head and, as if by magic, words appear on the page . . .

It's especially enjoyable to write poems because you can experiment with shape (the poem's visual form on the page), rhyme and rhythm. In this book I have tried to include poems with as much variety as possible in their style and subject matter.

Some of the poems are sad (like 'The Day After'), some are silly (like 'My Dog's First Poem'), some are spooky (like 'The Ghosts of The Grange'), some are serious (like 'Until Gran Died'), and some simply . . . sunny (like 'What is . . . the Sun?'). There are poems about creatures, characters, charms, cities and the countryside. As I write above – as much variety as possible.

Dip in and have a read, and – as they say in the USA – 'Enjoy!'

*Wes Magee*

# An Accident

The playground noise stilled.
A teacher ran to the spot
beneath the climbing frame
where Rawinda lay motionless.
We crowded around, silent,
gazing at the trickle of blood
oozing its way on to the tarmac.
Red-faced, the teacher shouted,
'Move back . . . get out of the way!'
and carried Rawinda into school,
limbs floppy as a rag doll's,
a red gash on her black face.

Later we heard she was at home,
five stitches in her forehead.
After school that day
Jane and I stopped beside the frame
and stared at the dark stain
shaped like a map of Ireland.
'Doesn't look much like blood,'
muttered Jane. I shrugged,
and remember now how warm it was
that afternoon, the white clouds,
and how sunlight glinted
from the polished bars.

Get
Well
Soon

We took Rawinda's 'Get Well' card
to her house. She was in bed,
quiet, propped up on pillows,
a white plaster on her dark skin.

Three days later
she was back at school,
her usual self, laughing,
twirling expertly on the bars,
wearing her plaster with pride,
covering for a week the scar
she would keep for ever,
memento of a July day at school.

# At the End of a School Day

It is the end of a school day
   and down the long driveway
come bag-swinging, shouting children.
   Deafened, the sky winces.
      The sun gapes in surprise.

Suddenly the runners skid to a stop,
   stand still and stare
at a small hedgehog
   curled-up on the tarmac
      like an old, frayed cricket ball.

A girl dumps her bag, tiptoes forward
   and gingerly, so gingerly,
carries the creature
   to the safety of a shady hedge.
      Then steps back, watching.

Girl, children, sky and sun
   hold their breath.
There is a silence,
   a moment to remember
      on this warm afternoon in June.

# I Like Emma

I like Emma
but I don't know
if she likes me.
All the boys
think I'm a fool.

I wait outside the school gate
at half past three
trying to keep my cool.
Emma walks past,
shaking her blonde hair free,
laughs with her friends
and drifts off home for tea.

Emma's two years
older than me.
Her class is higher
up the school.

I like Emma
but I don't know
if she likes me.
All the boys
think I'm a fool.

# Sunday Morning

Sunday morning
        and the Sun
        bawls
        with
        his big mouth.

Yachts
        paper triangles
        of white and blue
        crowd the sloping bay
        as if stuck there
        by some infant's thumb


        beneath a shouting sky


        upon a painted sea.

# The Spoons Music Man

My uncle
made music with spoons.

He could play
any number of tunes.

He banged them
on knees and his nose.

He banged them
on elbows and toes.

My uncle
made wonderful tunes.

He made
magical music with spoons.

# How to Reach the Sun . . . on a Sheet of Paper

Take a sheet of paper
and fold it.
Fold it again, and again, and again.
By the 6th fold
it is 1 centimetre thick.

fold to
reach ☀

By the 11th fold
it will be 32 centimetres thick,
and by the 15th fold
– 5 metres.

At the 24th fold
it is 2.5 kilometres,
and by fold 30
measures 160 kilometres high.

At the 35th fold
– 5,000 kilometres.
At the 43rd fold
it will reach to the Moon.

And by fold 52
it will stretch
from here
. . . to the Sun.

Take a sheet of paper.
Go on.
　　Try it!

# Coal Fire in December

It's great,
in icy December,
to get home
and chuck off
coat, gloves, boots,
scarf and
    hat.

And, *ah*,
sit in front of
a glowing coal fire
and hear
the warmth purr
like a contented
    cat.

# The Headmonster

A new headmaster arrives next week
  and rumours about him are rife.
They say he growls like a grizzly bear
  and that he chopped up his wife.

It's said he'll stride and stomp around school
  like a zombie in the night,
and that his icicle stare can freeze
  hundreds of children with fright.

It's rumoured he wears a skull-shaped ring,
  and a tie with nests of fleas.
When he smiles he shows razor-sharp fangs.
  There are tattoos on his knees.

We've heard that he has a werewolf's howl.
  There's a jagged scar on his cheek.
They say that he owns a whippy cane
  and that he'll use it next week.

Already he's called the 'The Headmonster'
  and some have named him 'The Ghoul'.
We'll soon find out if the rumours are true
  when he arrives at our school.

# Ripe

Across the Wolds
  fields are glut with rape,
marm rectangles
  of sun and butter.

Driving, we gloat
  over a landscape
gouached in gold:
  our ochrous season.

And there, below
  muscles of cumulus,
harvest's emblem
– a rainbow sharpens.

# The Child's Magic in the Gym

I cartwheel
past Changelings in the nut-brown wood.

I belly-crawl
when Witches fly to the yellow-faced Moon.

I forward roll
to escape the Werewolf's blood-red fangs.

I back-flip
as Ghosts gather in the dead-grey garden.

I vault the horse
if Bogeymen tap at the whitewashed windows.

I handstand
to confuse the Warlocks on the grass-green hill.

I freeze
when the Teacher's silver whistle sounds.

# My Dog's First Poem

*(to be read in a dog's voice)*

My barking drives them
up the wall.
I chew the carpet
in the hall.
I love to chase
a bouncing . . . banana?

Everywhere I leave
long hairs.
I fight the cushions
on the chairs.
Just watch me race
right up the . . . shower?

Once I chewed
a stick of chalk.
I get bored when
the family talk.
Then someone takes me
for a . . . wheelbarrow?

woof
woof
woof

# The Strangest School Secretary

She's Queen Wasp of the Office
　　and her throne's a swivel chair.
　　Her fingernails are purple.
　　　A wren nests in her hair.

　　Her eyes are green as seaweed
　　and she has a wildcat's stare.
　　She growls at timid teachers
just like a grizzly bear.

She makes inspectors nervous
　　and drives the parents spare.
　　　Headmaster, can't you sack her?
　　　You're right, he'd never dare!

　　Our secretary's the strangest.
　　She's really rather rare.
　　She's Queen Wasp of the Office
and her throne's a swivel chair.

# A Hard Winter

Not
a
twig
stirs.

The frost-bitten garden
huddles beneath
a heaped duvet of snow.

Pond,
tree,
sky
and
street

are granite with cold.

# An Evening

Crept in unseen, an evening.
On his back lawn a man stands.

The shrubbery holds its breath.
A fuchsia glows in the porch.

Leaves smoulder at garden ends.
Traffic, transistors murmur

almost below the threshold
of hearing. The sky deepens.

Lean from an upstairs window
and inhale this serene hour

before night climbs the Earth's curve
and the summer closes down.

Long may such moments endure
where the years pile and darken.

# Whoosh! Cheetah!

A member of the Cat family
      and sucH a speedy sprintah.
        It racEs across Africa's plains
to catch antelopE and zebrah.
    Can climb a Tree with agilitee,
       and is All quicksilver speed. A dashah.
Whoosh! CheetaH!

# Hiya, Cynth!

'Please mark my grave
with just one flower.'
That was the wish of
    Cynthia Tower.

So when she died
they raised a plinth
and marked upon it

    'Hiya, Cynth!'

# The Meadow in Midsummer

Immobilized by June heat
the chestnut trees
are calm cathedrals
      of bough and leaf.
In their deep shade
half-hidden horses
      seek relief.

The pond's azure eye
gazes amazed
at the gold coin
      dazzling the sky
as, barefoot amidst buttercups,
we cross the meadow,
      slowly pass by.

# The Tunneller

At number 42
there's a hawthorn perimeter hedge
and the front gate is topped
with strands of barbed wire.
The mad Major lives there,
a septuagenarian ex-soldier
with military moustache
and a broom-handle straight back.

On a mission,
in the last war, he parachuted into Germany,
was captured, and then held
in a prison camp: Stalag number 39.
He tunnelled out, escaped to England.
His true story is printed in a book
I found at the library:
*Spies of the Second World War.*

Yesterday,
at dusk, I hid in his long back garden
and spied on the Major
as he passed the old air-raid shelter
and marched into his garden shed.
He was dressed in black –
trousers, sweater, and woolly Balaclava.
Dirt streaks disguised his face.

I sneaked up
and through the cobwebby window
watched as the Major removed floorboards,
then lowered himself into a hole
and . . . disappeared!
He was tunnelling again,
digging beneath his back garden,
tunnelling towards the perimeter hedge.

An hour later
he emerged furtively from the shed
lugging a heavy sack
and I saw him scatter damp soil
between his rhubarb and cauliflowers.
Night after night he's at it,
secretly tunnelling his way to freedom,
trying to escape from Stalag number 42.

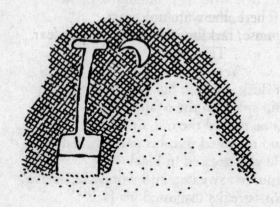

# Tiger Might

Tiger,
a creature of contrasts.

Here, just demanding to be stroked,
the velvety-soft striped fur coat.

There, which one huge raised paw
can strike dead gazelle, gnu or goat.

Tiger,
a creature of constrasts.

Here, the glinting eyes,
pools of shifting light. Tiger bright.

There, the watchful beast,
tense, lurking in shadows. Tiger fear.
Tiger might.

# A New Year

Night comes jackbooting through the wood
and the sky roars at trees and a dying light.
Pregnant, the river is gulped into darkness
while sheep, like town lights, blot out one by one.

In the house, beneath blanketing thatch,
twenty of us gather to see the New Year in.
We talk: wine runs away with itself
wailing demons are trapped up the chimney.

Midnight first-foots with a bombardment of snow.
The wind is celebrating madly.
Owls rattle in barns as we clasp hands
and another year is born in a blitz of stars.

*(Totleigh Barton, Devon)*

# The Ghosts of 'The Grange'

Miss Starvelling-Stamper died in 'twenty-four.
They found her stone-cold on the flagstoned floor.

She lay beside the kitchen's cast-iron range,
last Starvelling-Stamper to dwell at 'The Grange'.

Since then the mansion's been abandoned, locked:
its windows smashed, roof collapsed, sewers blocked.

The croquet lawn's been lost to Queen Anne's lace.
'The Grange' is now a sad, forgotten place.

Yet, nightly ghosts creep from each crumbling wall
and gather in the leaf-strewn marble hall

– a chambermaid drifts up the woodwormed stairs,
a skivvy flicks at cobwebs on the chairs,

two snooty butlers wait where moonbeams slant,
see there a grim and gaunt tiaraed aunt.

Miss Starvelling-Stamper's ghost – last of the line –
lifts to her lips a goblet of French wine

and floats above the kitchen's flagstoned floor
where she was found stone-cold in 'twenty-four.

# Afraid of the Dark?

Not me. I like the dark
and the way it closes round me
like a big friendly duvet
after they've said, 'Goodnight,
sleep tight, watch the bugs don't bite!'
and switched off my bedroom light.
Then I lie in the darkness
listening to sounds outside.
Someone shouts. A dog barks.
A motorbike roars past, changes gear,
and fades into the distance
as I slowly drop

off
to
sleep . . .

It's *then* I grow scared.
The nightmares overwhelm me.
In one I'm clinging
to the mane of a runaway horse.
We jump a ditch, leap a thick hedge,
but at the stone wall I'm thrown.
I fall . . . fall . . . fall . . .
In another I'm alone
at the wheel of a racing car.
The brakes fail. The car speeds
towards a deep and gloomy lake.
Splash! And I go

down
down
down . . .

I wake, sweating with fright.
My bedside clock shows 2.00 a.m.
The house is silent as the grave.
I stare into the thrumming night
and the darkness calms me.
The nightmares shrink and sink
into the centre of my skull.

I lie there, the darkness soothing
– like Mum's hand on my forehead
when I was ill with the flu,
and quietly, gently
and slowly I drop
                    off
                        to
                            sleep . . .

# City Sounds Heard after Dark

The sweesh sweesh of speeding cars.
  Old songs from the crowded bars.
    Disco drums and loud guitars.

Aircraft zapping through the sky.
  Rooftop cats that spit and cry.
    Laughter from the passers-by.

Motorbikers' sudden roar.
  Corner lads who josh and jaw.
    A call. A shout. A slammed door.

The guard dogs that howl and bark.
  Voices from the padlocked park.
    City sounds heard after dark.

# The Witch's Brew

Hubble bubble at the double
Cooking pot stir up some trouble.

Into my pot
there now must go
leg of lamb
and green frog's toe,

old men's socks
and dirty jeans,
a rotten egg
and cold baked beans.

Hubble bubble at the double
Cooking pot stir up some trouble.

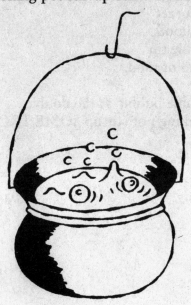

One dead fly
and a wild wasp's sting,
the eye of a sheep
and the heart of a king,

a stolen jewel
and mouldy salt,
and for good flavour
a jar of malt.

> Hubble bubble at the double
> Cooking pot stir up some trouble.

Wing of bird
and head of mouse,
screams and howls
from the Haunted House,

and don't forget
the jug of blood,
or the sardine tin
and the clod of mud.

> Hubble bubble at the double
> Cooking pot stir up SOME TROUBLE!

# Down There on the Corner

Down there on the corner
at the far end of the street
hear the chatter and the patter
and the sound of stamping feet
to a blaster that is pounding out
a really funky beat
        down there on the corner
                where the young bloods meet.

Down there on the corner
at the far end of the street
watch the hoppers and the boppers
and the dressers looking neat
as they toe-tap to the rhythms
of a throbbing sound that's sweet
        down there on the corner
                where the young bloods meet.

Down there on the corner
at the far end of the street
all the teenies and the weenies
do the high fives when they greet
while the music's coolly thumping
through the summer's dust and heat
        down there on the corner
                where the young bloods meet.

# He Loves Me, He Loves Me Not . . .

It's hot, sweltering, as children
spill from the school at lunchtime
and spread across the field.
> Friday. Sun-high noon.
> It's the last day
> of heatwave June.

With legs splayed
three girls sit and pick daisies.
They must endure Sports Day
> all that long, hot afternoon.
> For them the summer holidays
> can't come too soon.

> 'He loves me,
> he loves me not,
> he loves me,
> he loves me not . . .'

It's a massacre.
Around the girls lie daisies
by the score,
> dying in the heat-stunned air.
> The sun's unblinking eye
> is a fierce glare.

The girls chant lazily
dreaming who'll be the one
to get lucky with Richard,
     the boy with flame-red hair.
     Will it be Emma,
     Anne-Marie, or Claire?

     'He loves me,
     he loves me not,
     he loves me,
     he loves me not . . .'

# The Peasants' Revolt, 1381

There was a grumbling in the land
and soon the peasants were revolting.
> In their hordes they massed for battle
> but, alas, smelled just like cattle.
> Most were dandruffy and toothless
> as in rags they fought the ruthless.
> The poor peasants, pocked-marked, potty,
> were all scabby-legged and spotty.
The came in cartloads, sick with jolting.
Oh yes,
the peasants were revolting.

There was a mumbling in the land
and soon the peasants were revolting.
> Armed with scythes and pitchforks (rusty),
> they were dirty, drunk and dusty.
> Grimy hands hurled stones and boulders.
> Nitty hair hung to their shoulders.
> The sad peasants, squint-eyed, shabby,
> were as thin as rakes, or flabby.
Their goatskin coats were patched, some moulting.
Oh yes,
the peasants were revolting.

# Down by the School Gate

There goes the bell,
it's half past three
and down by the school gate
you will see . . .

       ten mums talk talk talking
       nine babies squawk squawking
       eight toddlers all squabbling
       seven grans on bikes, wobbling

       six dogs bark bark barking
       five cars stopping, parking
       four child-minders running
       three bus drivers sunning

       two teenagers dating
       one lollipop man waiting . . .

The school is out,
it's half past three
and the first to the school gate
is . . . me!

# The Boneyard Rap

This is the rhythm
of the boneyard rap,
knuckle bones click
and hand bones clap,
finger bones flick
and thigh bones slap,
when you're doing the rhythm
of the boneyard rap.
Woooooooooo!

It's the boneyard rap
and it's a scare.
Give your bones a shake-up
if you dare.
Rattle your teeth
and waggle your jaw
and let's do the boneyard rap
once more.

This is the rhythm
of the boneyard rap,
elbow bones clink
and backbones snap,
shoulder bones chink
and toe bones tap,
when you're doing the rhythm
of the boneyard rap.
Woooooooooo!

It's the boneyard rap
and it's a scare.
Give your bones a shake-up
if you dare.
Rattle your teeth
and waggle your jaw
and let's do the boneyard rap
once more.

This is the rhythm
of the boneyard rap,
ankle bones sock
and arm bones flap,
pelvic bones knock
and knee bones zap,
when you're doing the rhythm
of the boneyard rap.
  Wooooooooo!

# A Day in the Hills

They went for a picnic
in the hills.
The sun blazed golden
in a shimmering blue sky.
   'My, it's hot!'
   'It's the hottest day yet!'

They flew a kite,
ran through long grass,
then picnicked beside a stream,
a bone-dry, stone-dry stream.
   'It's the drought.'
   'There's been no rain for weeks.'

No cool pools.
No water falling over rocks.
No fish.
No birds.
No sound.

Now, in winter,
they remember that day in the hills,
remember the golden sun, blue sky,
the picnic, but most of all
   that bone-dry, stone-dry,
   still and sadly silent stream.

# The Waterfall

Over the rugged rocks
the
     w
     a
     t
     e
     r
     f
     a
     l
     l
             tumbles
              and rumbles.

In winter
it gasps,
groans
  and grumbles.

But in summer
it's quiet.
It whispers
  and mumbles.

# Faraway Places

Faraway places
are calling to me,
calling to me
  over land,
    over sea.
Snow-mufflered Moscow,
the frozen South Pole,
east to Kyoto,
and Hong Kong, and Seoul.
Dripping wet jungles,
vast African plain,
north to Yakutsk
by Siberian train.
Matterhorn mountain,
adrift on the Med.

Nights in the desert
with stars overhead.
Trekking the Outback,
exploring Vietnam,
up the Grand Canyon,
to Grand Coulee Dam.
Outer Mongolia
and Island Magee,
faraway places
are calling to me.
Lake Titicaca,
Belize, and Bel-Air,
Kabul, Kurdistan,
and County Kildare.
Faraway places
are calling to me,
calling me there
   over land,
      over sea.
Faraway places
are calling me there,
the sun on my face,
the wind in my hair.
Faraway places
are calling me,
   calling me,
      calling me there.

# Miss Jones, Football Teacher

Miss Jones
  football teacher
red shellsuit
  flash boots.
She laughs
  as she dribbles,
shrieks, 'GOAL!'
  when she
    shoots.

Miss Jones
  what a creature
pink lipstick
  shin pads.
See there
  on the touchline
lines of
  drooling
    lads.

Miss Jones
  finest feature
long blonde hair
– it's neat!
She 'bend' kicks
  and back-heels,
she's fast
  on her
    feet.

Miss Jones
   football teacher
told us, 'don't
   give up!'
She made us
   train harder,
and we
   won the
      Cup!

# Climb the Mountain

```
        see      t
      blow,      h
       you       e
    against
      wind       f
       the       i
      Feel       e
      sky.       l
      the        d
      see        s
      and
    clouds       f
      the        a
    touch        r
    high,        f
  mountain       a
     the         r
    climb        b
   Climb         e
                 l
                 o
                 w.
```

# The Girl in the Graveyard

In early spring she's seen
flitting through the graveyard, tresses flowing.
She shelters from an April shower
in the lee of a mossed stone wall,
and is startled
when pigeons rise from the church tower
and flap away into the blue.
        But who is she, who?

        Why she comes
        and where she goes
        no one knows
        no one knows.

Barefoot in summer she's seen
treading between the tombstones
as the tower clock dully strikes one.
Swallows describe perfect arcs
in the insect-laden air
as she seeks shade from July's sun
beneath the dark foliage of a yew.
        But who is she, who?

        Why she comes
        and where she goes
        no one knows
        no one knows.

In September she's seen
kneeling beside an unmarked grave,
a red rose clutched in her hand.

Leaves spiral down
as rooks caw and circle above the elms.
When thunder rumbles across the land
she departs leaving footprints in the dew.
But who is she, who?

Why she comes
and where she goes
no one knows
no one knows.

Shawled in December she's seen
slipping through the lych-gate
as heavy snow falls.
A robin's perched on a leaning headstone
as she waits, shivering,
beside the church tower's icy walls
perhaps recalling someone she once knew.
But who is she, who?

Why she comes
and where she goes
no one knows
no one knows.

# Guard Wolf in Siberia

My coat is thick,
my teeth are strong,
the snow lies deep,
the winter's long.

I stand on guard
here in the cold.
The pack's asleep.
Some grow old.
I live by hunting.
Men hunt me.
When guns spit fire
we run, we flee.

My coat is thick,
my teeth are strong,
the snow lies deep,
the winter's long.

In fairy tales
I roamed the wood,
the bad wolf in
'Red Riding Hood'.
If I howl now
the pack will wake.
We'll flee across
the frozen lake.

My coat is thick,
my teeth are strong,
the snow lies deep,
the winter's long.

# It's Christmas Time!

Carols drift across the night
Holly gleams by candlelight
Roaring fire; a spooky tale
Ice and snow and wind and hail
Santa seen in High Street store
Television . . . more and *more*
Mince pies, turkey, glass of wine
Acting your own pantomime
Socks hung up. It's Christmas time!

# The Day After

I went to school
the day after Dad died.
Teacher knew all about it.
She put a hand on my shoulder
   and sighed.

In class things seem much the same
although I felt strangely subdued.
Playtime was the same too,
and at lunchtime the usual crew
played-up the dinner supervisors.
Fraggle was downright rude.
I joined in the football game

but volunteered to go in goal.
That way I was left almost alone,
could think things over on my own.
For once I let the others shout
   and race and roll.

\*   \*   \*   \*

First thing that afternoon,
everyone in his and her place
for silent reading,
I suddenly felt hot tears streaming
   down my face.

Salty tears splashed down
and soaked into my book's page.
Sobs heaved in my chest.
Teacher peered over her half specs
and said quietly, 'Ben, come here.'
I stood at her desk, crying. At my age!
I felt like an idiot, a clown.

'Don't feel ashamed,' teacher said.
'It's only right to weep.
Here, have these tissues to keep.'
I dabbed my eyes, then looked around.
  Bowed into books, every head.

*   *   *   *

'Have a cold drink.
Go with James. He'll understand.'
In the boys' cloaks I drank deeply
then slowly wiped my mouth
  on the back of my hand.

Sheepishly I said, 'My dad died.'
'I know,' said James.
'We'd best get back to class. Come on.'
Walking down the corridor I thought of Dad . . . gone.
In class no one sniggered,
they were busy getting changed for games.
No one noticed I'd cried.

All day I felt sad, sad.
After school I reached my street,
clutching the tissues, dragging my feet.
Mum was there in our house,
    but no Dad, no Dad.

# When the Chimney Sweep Calls

It's September
when the chimney sweep calls,
his face and overalls smudged.
He kneels in the fireplace
and removes last winter's soot
          from our chimney.
The hoovering machine whines.
Smut floats in the air
and you sniff that sweet scent
          of powder-soft soot.

          The job's soon done
and our chimney's cleaned
ready for the coming winter.
There'll be fire in the grate –
blazing logs, glowing coal,
          and swirling smoke.
Then, silently and secretly,
soot will gather up the chimney
and lie there until September
          when the chimney sweep calls.

# At the End of World War Two

To celebrate the end of the war
all the lads and lasses
have gathered at the thistly meadow
for a twenty-five-a-side football match.

The unmarked pitch slopes down
to a duckweed-covered pond
where muddied cattle drink.
White goats crop the hawthorn.

Goalposts are heaped jackets,
waistcoats and flat caps.
The ball's a pig's bladder,
inflated, and tied with twine.

Endless, the game thunders on,
on into the gloaming.
The score is nineteen-all
as the purple dusk deepens.

There are only two spectators
in the bomber-free sky:
an invalid-faced full Moon
and a single astonished star.

# Morning Break

Andrew Flag plays football
Jane swings from the bars
Chucker Peach climbs drainpipes
Spike is seeing stars

Little Paul's a Martian
Anne walks on her toes
Ian Dump fights Kenny
Russell picks his nose

Dopey Di plays hopscotch
Curly drives a train
Maddox-Brown and Lai Ching
Stuff shoes down the drain

Lisa Thin throws netballs
Tanji stands and stares
Nuttall from the first year
Shouts and spits and swears

Nick Fish fires his ray gun
Gaz has stamps to swap
Dave and Dan are robbers
Teacher is the cop

Betty Blob pulls faces
Basher falls . . . and cries
Tracey shows her knickers
Loony swallows flies

Faye sits in a puddle
Trevor's eating mud
Skinhead has a nosebleed
– pints and pints of blood

Robbo Lump pings marbles
Ahmed hands out cake
It's all a lot of nonsense
      During
            Morning
                  Break.

# Our Miss Gill and Mr Scott

Our Miss Gill
and Mr Scott
seem to like each other
rather a lot.
His class
and our class
are always going
on trips together.
Today we climbed
Tucker's Hill
in *dreadful* weather.
       'He held her hand.'
              'Never!'
       'He did. And they kissed.'
              'No!'
It turned terribly cold.
       'I'm freezing,' said Jill.
It started to rain,
then there was sleet,
and then there was snow.

At least it was warm
on the coach,
and we all sang.
Arrived back at the school gate
just as the bell rang.
Off we trooped home.
At the street corner
I turned
and looked back.
So did Jill.

We watched
as our Miss Gill
crossed the car park
hand in glove
with Mr Scott.
          'They *are* in love,' said Jill.
Yes, they do seem
to like each other
rather a lot.

# The Slime Beasts

deep
down
in the darkness
of an octopus-ocean
deep
down
in the squid-ridden
sharkery sea
the
slime beasts
are mating
the
slime beasts
are waiting
for
the end of the world
and for you
and for
me

                deep
                down
        in the mudmurk
        of an oyster-squashed ocean
                deep
                down
        in the skate-smelly
        sandsquishy sea
                the
                slime beasts
                aren't sleeping
                the slime beasts
                are creeping
                to
        the end of the world
        and for you
                and for
                        me

deep
down
in the inkpitch
of an ooze-boozy ocean
deep
down
in the seaweedy
shipwreck-strewn sea
the
slime beasts
are slumming
the slime beasts
are coming
it's
the end of the world
and for you
and for
me

# Sparkler

A magic stick,
  Guy Fawkes' wand,
    held tight
      in a thick-gloved hand.

Blooming at night
  a rose from Mars:
    the 'Fizzer',
      my 'Maker of Stars'.

# Giant Rocket

A moonshot falling short

it bursts
in a shower
of stars
then spirals
down
to distant trees,
an ember
d
y
i
n
g

# Remembering Dinosaurs

Years ago, on a drizzly day,
my uncle drove me across southern England
      until we arrived at
an abandoned quarry near Lyme Regis.
'Just the day for dinosaurs,' he quipped
      as I lugged on wellies and bobble hat.

Plodding through that muddy moonscape
we found fossilized footprints
      stomped by dinosaurs epochs ago.
'Stegosaurus walked this way,' Uncle joked
as he waddled along the path
      chortling like a half-crazed crow.

Further on we spotted petrified eggs,
exposed, and big as footballs.
        Uncle cracked, 'Boil me those for breks!'
and made me grin that grey day.
Overhead, thunder bellowed and boomed.
        'Hey up! Here comes Tyrannosaurus Rex!'

Years ago, yet I remember that visit
and the dinosaur names he taught me
        – Diplodocus, Triceratops, Dimetrodon.
He made a damp day bright,
remains stamped on my memory
        even though, like the dinosaurs,
                he's long, long gone.

# A Week of Winter Weather

On Monday icy rains poured down
and flooded drains all over town.

Tuesday's gales bashed elm and ash:
dead branches came down with a crash.

On Wednesday bursts of hail and sleet.
No one walked along our street.

Thursday stood out clear and calm
but the sun was paler than my arm.

Friday's frost that bit your ears
was cold enough to freeze your tears.

Saturday's sky was ghostly grey:
we smashed ice on the lake today.

Christmas Eve was Sunday . . . and
snow fell like foam across the land.

# Up on the Downs

Up on the Downs,
Up on the Downs,
A skylark flutters
And the fox barks shrill.
Brown rabbit scutters
And the hawk hangs still.
Up on the Downs,
Up on the Downs,
With butterflies
jigging
like
costumed
clowns.

Here in the Hills,
Here in the Hills,
The long grass flashes
And the sky seems vast.
Rock lizard dashes
And a crow flies past.
Here in the Hills,
Here in the Hills,
With bumble bees
buzzing
like
high-speed
drills.

High on the Heath,
High on the Heath,
The slow-worm slithers
And the trees are few.
Fieldmouse dithers
And the speedwell's blue.
High on the Heath,
High on the Heath,
Where the grasshoppers
chirp
in the
grass
beneath.

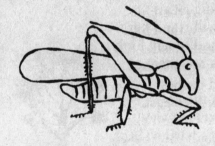

# Tracey's Tree

Last year it was not there,
the sapling with purple leaves
planted in our school grounds with care.
It's Tracey's tree, my friend who died,
and last year it was not there.

Tracey the girl with long black hair,
who, out playing one day, ran
across a main road for a dare.
The lorry struck her. Now a tree grows
and last year it was not there.

Through the classroom window I stare
and watch the sapling sway.
Soon its branches will stand bare.
It wears a forlorn and lonely look
and last year it was not there.

October's chill is in the air
and cold rain distorts my view.
I feel a sadness that's hard to bear.
The trees blurs, as if I've been crying,
and last year it was not there.

# A British Garden

The SPRING garden is *Irish* green,
its forty shades ranging
from the emerald stems of tulips
to the lawn's striped lemon and lime.
Already the garden is looking spruce,
a daffodil buttonhole on its jacket.
At gloaming see the crocus candles,
tiny flames of azure and crimson.

The SUMMER garden is *Welsh* dragon-red,
roses vivid as blood blots in the borders
while sunflowers beam down on leeks.
We lie beneath leafy trees slowly toasting,
first salmon-pink then lobster.
Red hot pokers stoke up the heat.
At evening look westward,
see how the sky runs with cochineal.

The AUTUMN garden is *Scots* tartan,
a blend of russet, gold and blue.
The trees wear plaid overcoats.
Soon bonfires at garden ends,
then skirls of smoke, kilts of flame.
The clans gather for roast chestnuts,
watch fireworks shed their silver stars.
The children squeal and screech like bagpipes.

The WINTER garden is *English* white,
a cool bride who prepares herself
from a ceremony of pure cold.
Her snow gown dazzles with frost sequins.
The garden waterfall is iced like a
many-tiered wedding cake. A silence,
before the guest celebrate.
Children hurl white meringues against walls.

# Who?

'Who,' asked my mother,
'helped themselves to the new loaf?'
    My two friends and I
    looked at her
    and shrugged.

'Who,' questioned my mother,
'broke off the crust?'
    Three pairs of eyes
    stared at the loaf
    lying on the kitchen table.

'Who,' demanded my mother,
'ate the bread?'
    No one replied.
    You could hear
    the kitchen clock. Tick. Tock.

And
even now I can taste it,
crisp, fresh, warm from the bakery,
    and I'd eat it again
    if I could find a loaf
    like that,
             like that . . .

# Football! Football!

Football! *Football*!
The boys want the entire playground
and we're left squashed
against the broken fence.
Why don't the teachers stop them?
   Why?
Haven't they got *any* sense?

   My friend Emma
ran across the tarmac. Smack!
Got the football right on her nose.
Blood all over her face.
Why don't the teachers do something?
   Why?
It's a disgrace, a *disgrace*!

   Those boys . . . I mean
they're like hooligans.
CHEL-SEA! CHEL-SEA! they chant
morning, noon and night.
The teacher on duty does . . . nothing.
   Why?
It's just . . . it's just not right!

   We complain bitterly
but the duty teacher says,
'Go and see the Head. He's in charge.'
Him! He useless! YOU-ESS-LESS!
When we ask him to ban football,
   why,
oh why, can't he just say, 'Yes'?

# A Charm for Sweet Dreams

May the Ghost
  lie in its grave.
May the Vampire
  see the light.
May the Witch
  keep to her cave,
and the Spectre
  melt from sight.

May the Wraith
  stay in the Wood.
May the Banshee
  give no fright.
May the Ghoul
  be gone for good,
and the Zombie
  haste its flight.

May the Troll
  no more be seen.
May the Werewolf
  lose its bite.
May all Spooks
  and Children Green
fade for ever
    in
      the
        night . . .

# Counting Sheep

They said,
'If you can't get to sleep
  try counting sheep.'
I tried.
It didn't work.

They said,
'Still awake? Count rabbits, dogs
  or leaping frogs.'
I tried.
It didn't work.

They said,
'It's *very* late. Count rats
  or vampire bats!'
I tried.
It didn't work.

They said,
'Stop counting stupid sheep!
*Eyes closed*! *Don't peep*!'
I tried,

and fell asleep.

# Exploring the Deserted Mansion

In the hall . . .
cobwebs hang from the crumbling ceiling,
antlered hatstand's carved from oak,
crimson carpet's tattered and torn
and dust in the air makes you choke.
  Chilly,
  icy mansion.
  Dank,
  deserted place.

In the kitchen . . .
tarnished taps drip brackish water,
stale loaf's grown a coat of mould,
a foul stench seeps up from the drain
and the radiators feel stone cold.
  Fusty,
  foetid mansion.
  Damp,
  deserted place.

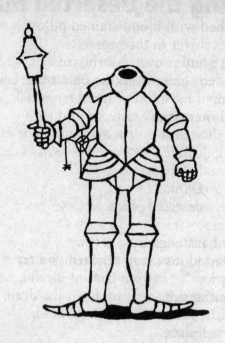

On the landing . . .
a headless, rusty suit of armour,
ancient portrait's green eyes glare,
cracked mirror in a silver frame
and rat bones on the rocking chair.
    Echoing,
    creaky mansion.
    Dark,
    deserted place.

In the bedroom . . .
a tousled bed with blood-stained pillow,
rent drapes shiver in the breeze,
cockroach scuttles over floorboards
and a sudden screech makes you freeze.
Faded,
pallid mansion.
Dim,
deserted place.

Up in the attic . . .
frayed dressing gowns have nests of mice,
there's Santa's sack for Christmas Eve,
a vampire bat hangs from a beam
and the trapdoor's jammed when you try to leave . . .
Creepy,
scary mansion.
Dead,
deserted place.

# The House on the Hill

It was built years ago
by someone quite manic
and sends those who go there
away in blind panic.
They tell tales of horrors
that can injure or kill
designed by the madman
who lived on the hill.

If you visit the House on the Hill for a dare
remember my words . . . 'There are dangers.
Beware!'

The piano's white teeth
when you plonk out a note
will bite off your fingers
then reach for your throat.
The living-room curtains
– long, heavy, and black –
will wrap you in cobwebs
if you're slow to step back.

If you visit the House on the Hill for a dare
remember my words . . . 'There are dangers.
Beware!'

The fridge in the kitchen
has a self-closing door.
If it knocks you inside
then you're ice cubes . . . for sure.
The steps to the cellar
are littered with bones,
and up from the darkness
drift creakings and groans.

> If you visit the House on the Hill for a dare
> remember my words . . . 'There are dangers.
> Beware!'

Turn on the hot tap
and the bathroom will flood
not with gallons of water
but litres of blood.
The rocking chair's arms
can squeeze you to death.
It's a waste of time shouting
as you run . . . out . . . of . . . breath.

> Don't say you weren't warned or told to take
> care
> when you entered the House on the Hill . . .
> for a dare.

# Until Gran Died

The minnows I caught
lived for a few days in a jar
then floated side-up on the surface.
We buried them beneath the hedge.
I didn't cry.
but felt sad inside.

     I thought
     I could deal with funerals
     that is
     until Gran died.

The goldfish I kept in a bowl
passed away with old age.
Mum wrapped him in a newspaper
and we buried him next to a rose bush.
I didn't cry,
but felt sad inside.

     I thought
     I could deal with funerals
     that is
     until Gran died.

My cat lay stiff in a shoebox
after being hit by a car.
Dad dug a hole and we buried her
under the apple tree.
I didn't cry,
but felt *very* sad inside.

I thought
I could deal with funerals
that is
until Gran died.

And when she died
I went to the funeral
with relations dressed in black.
They cried, and so did I.
Salty tears ran down my face.
Oh, how I cried.

Yes, I thought
I could deal with funerals
that is
until Gran died.

She was buried in a graveyard
and even the sky wept that day.
Rain fell and fell and fell
and thunder sobbed far away across the town.
I cried
and I cried.

I thought
I could deal with funerals
that is
until Gran died.

# In the Misty, Murky Graveyard

In the misty, murky graveyard
      there's a midnight dance,
and in moonlight shaking skeletons
are twirling in a trance.
Linked arm in bony arm
they point and pitch and prance,
down there in the graveyard
      at the midnight dance.

In the misty, murky graveyard
      there's a midnight rave,
and a score of swaying skeletons
are lurching round a grave.
Their toe bones tip and tap
and their rattling fingers wave,
down there in the graveyard
      at the midnight rave.

In the misty, murky graveyard
      there's a midnight romp,
and the squad of skinless skeletons
all quiver as they stomp.
To the whistle of the wind
they clink and clank and clomp,
down there in the graveyard
      at the midnight romp.

# Announcing the Guests at the Space Beasts' Party

'The Araspew from Bashergrannd'
'The Cakkaspoo from Danglebannd'
'The Eggisplosh from Ferrintole'
'The Gurglenosh from Hiccupole'
'The Inkiblag from Jupitickle'
'The Kellogclag from Lamandpickle'
'The Mighteemoose from Nosuchplace'
'The Orridjuice from Piggiface'
'The Quizziknutt from Radishratt'
'The Spattersplut from Trikkicatt'
'The Underpance from Verristrong'
'The Willidance from Xrayblong'
'The Yuckyspitt from Ziggersplitt'

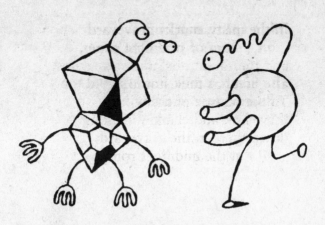

# What is . . . the Sun?

The Sun is an orange dinghy
  sailing across a calm sea.

It is a gold coin
  dropped down the drain in Heaven.

The Sun is a yellow beach ball
  kicked high into the summer sky.

It is a red thumbprint
  on a sheet of pale blue paper.

The Sun is a milk bottle's gold top
  floating in a puddle.

# The Cat with No Name

In the dingy staffroom of a school in the city,
where the teachers' damp macs hang limply from hooks,
where cracked cups are tea-stained, the worn carpet gritty,
and where there are piles of exercise books,
you will notice – at break – that the teachers don't utter
a sound. None of them grumble and none of them chat.
Why? They dare not disturb what sleeps, fat as butter,
on the staffroom's best chair: one huge tortoiseshell cat.

> For the teachers
> know very well not to wake him.
> They know that he's three parts not tame.
> He's a wild cat,
> a *wild* cat,
> a not-to-be-riled cat.
> He's the tortoiseshell cat with no name.

It was drizzly December when the cat first appeared
and took the French teacher's chair for his bed.
Now his scimitar claws in the staffroom are feared,
oh yes, and the street-fighter's teeth in his head.
Once a day he is seen doing arches and stretches,
then for hours like a furry coiled fossil will lie.
It's true that he's made all the staff nervous wretches.
They approach . . . and he opens one basilisk eye.

For the teachers
know very well not to stroke him.
They know that he'll not play the game.
He's a wild cat,
a *wild* cat,
a not-to-be-riled cat.
He's the tortoiseshell cat with no name.

The Headmistress, the teachers, and all the school's
   cleaners
can't shift him with even a long-handled broom,
for the cat merely yawns, treats them all like has-beeners
and continues to live in that dingy staffroom.
When the French teacher tried to reclaim her armchair
with a cat-cally, shriek-squally, 'Allez-vous-en!',
the cat gave a hiss, clawed the lady's long hair,
and back to Marseilles Madame Toff-Pouff has gone.

For the teachers
know very well not to irk him.
They know that he's always the same.
He's a wild cat,
a *wild* cat,
a not-to-be-riled cat.
He's the tortoiseshell cat with no name.

I once worked in that school and observed the huge creature's
habits as I sipped my cracked cup of weak tea.
I saw how he frightened and flummoxed the teachers,
    and how – every Friday – he'd one-green-eye me.
To appease him, each day we laid out a fish dinner
    which the beast snaffled-up in just one minute flat
then returned to his chair with a smirk – the bad sinner!
    It seems there's no way to be rid of that cat.

        For the teachers
        know very well not to cross him.
        They know that he's three parts not tame.
        He's a wild cat,
        a *wild* cat,
        a not-to-be-riled cat.
        (He can't bear to be smiled at).
        He's the tortoiseshell cat with no name,
        with no name.
        He's the tortoiseshell cat with no name.

# Index of First Lines

# The very best poetry available from Macmillan

The prices shown below are correct at the time of going to press. However, Macmillan Publishers reserve the right to show new retail prices on covers which may differ from those previously advertised.

| | | |
|---|---|---|
| **The Very Best of Richard Edwards** | 0 330 39389 8 | £3.99 |
| **The Very Best of Ian McMillan** | 0 330 39365 0 | £3.99 |
| **The Very Best of Vernon Scannell** | 0 330 48344 7 | £3.99 |
| **The Very Best of Paul Cookson** | 0 330 48014 6 | £3.99 |
| **The Very Best of David Harmer** | 0 330 48190 8 | £3.99 |
| **The Very Best of Wes Magee** | 0 330 48192 4 | £3.99 |

All Macmillan titles can be ordered at your local bookshop or are available by post from:

**Book Service by Post**
**PO Box 29, Douglas, Isle of Man IM99 1BQ**

Credit cards accepted. For details:
Telephone: 01624 675137
Fax: 01624 670923
E-mail: bookshop@enterprise.net

**Free postage and packing in the UK.**
Overseas customers: add £1 per book (paperback)
and £3 per book (hardback).